*Snatch Back Your
Personal Power*

*"Learn to Increase Your
Spiritual and Moral
Strength"*

***ANDREA FREEMAN***

Copyright©2017 Andrea Freeman

All Rights Reserved. No part of this book may be reproduced or transmitted in any form or by any means, electronic or mechanical, including photocopying, recording, or by any information storage and retrieval system, without prior written permission from the Author/Publisher of this book, except for the inclusion of brief quotations in printed reviews.

Scriptures taken from MSG, NIV, AMP Version Bible

ISBN: 978-0-692-86299-5

Published in U.S. by Changing Lives And Sincerely Supporting You, Inc.

# *Contents*

Dedication……………………………5

***Chapter One***
Do I Really Have Personal Power?..…6

***Chapter Two***
The Blame Game………………...……12

***Chapter Three***
Pitiful or Powerful……………………22

***Chapter Four***
Your Greatest Enemy…………………30

***Chapter Five***
Unshackle Your Perspective…….…...39

***Chapter Six***
Think About What You Are Thinking About……………………………….…45

***Chapter Seven***
Accept and Validate Yourself……..……54

***Chapter Eight***
Who's The Judge?...............................66

***Chapter Nine***
Much Power Lies Within Your Mental Strength…………………………………73

***Chapter Ten***
Appreciate Being Who God Created You To Be…………………………………….79

***Contact The Author***……………..……84

*This book is dedicated to all of my supporters and readers, whom I appreciate beyond any words. It is my prayer that you walk in your God assigned greatness, and live the life of your dreams. I thank you for keeping me lifted in prayer, encouraging and inspiring me to move to greater levels and never to give up. You are my reason to continue striving to be the best that I can be. Without you, there is no reason for me to constantly pick up my pen and paper. Thank you all. I love you very much.*

# Chapter 1
## _Do I Really Have Personal Power?_

Having personal power is having the ability to lead yourself freely and change the direction of your life. If you can visualize being at your absolute best and having the ability to manifest your inner world, you can possess personal power and benefit from it.

When you possess personal power, you can be authentically you and use your God given gifts in a way that makes you happy. You have the ability to create conditions where your ambition, aspirations, and beliefs all connect. You have the ability to find the blessing in every experience, good or bad.

Your personal power comes from having a strong sense of who you are. How you feel, think, and your opinion of yourself are all a part of your personal power. It consists of being confident enough to act on your known gifts and talents.

Your personal power starts with your family origin. Your family was the starting point with their way of thinking and doing things. Your family members were the first people to tell you who they thought you were and what they thought you were and were not capable of doing.

Who you are is always connected to your personal power because you communicate or show your sense of self in what you do and what you do discloses who you think you are. In describing yourself and choosing reactions on your own definition of who you are, you were either helped or hindered by your family's willingness or unwillingness to allow you to act on your own.

However, if your family struggled seeing you apart from them, if they wanted who you are to serve the needs of who they are, they may not have been able to help you to grow your self-esteem, self-determination, and creativity. If your parents experienced any unpleasant or unsettled issues in those areas, it made it harder for them to encourage you and help develop your personal power.

The good news is that you don't have to allow past family experiences to impede your ability to stand on your own today. You can still strengthen your personal power on your own. Your powerful inner spirit can help you if it's further released and empowered.

One of the most effective ways to grow or snatch back your personal power is to refrain from agreeing with any negative or sabotaging thought of who your family said you would be based on issues that they have within themselves. Practice focusing your attention on positive things so that you may navigate through difficult situations. Don't allow yourself to be put down and convinced that you have failed and don't possess the self- discipline or willpower to succeed.

It's also important to break energy wasting habits that don't serve you. Some of the things you are focusing on can be mere distractions and need to be eliminated in order for you to gain or recover your personal power. Avoid expending your personal power on things that exhaust you so that you can create your life in a way that you choose.

Exercise your personal power, accept your decisions, move in the direction you desire, and take control of your own life. When you do this, you have the authority and freedom to give yourself permission to achieve whatever you wish. Your power will begin to grow and your chances of succeeding will increase.

You must have the confidence and courage to use your personal power because it only exists if you use it.


**(Luke 10:19 AMP)** "Listen carefully: I have given you authority [that you now possess] to tread on [a]serpents and scorpions, and [the ability to exercise authority] over all the power of the enemy (Satan); and nothing will [in any way] harm you."

## **Chapter Checkpoint:**

What have you been told by others, that has negatively affected your inner confidence?


What will make you feel more in control of how you lead your life?


How do you navigate through difficult situations?


What do you do to exercise your personal power?

# Chapter 2
## *The Blame Game*

Throughout life we experience many different challenges. The challenges are usually very uncomfortable, and we look for ways to lessen our pain by making excuses or blaming others for the trouble we have made in our own lives. Little do we know that excuses and blaming are just defense mechanisms employed by our minds that help to protect our self-image.

Making excuses and blaming always makes sense to the person doing it. It's less demanding when we don't accept personal responsibility and it allows us to give up control of a situation to help our egos feel a little bit better. Taking responsibility often makes one feel powerless and the ego doesn't like feeling powerless one bit.

What we fail to realize is that when we don't accept responsibility, we pay a high price of creating and empowering a victim mentality and giving up our power to change. When we give up our power, we have no control or influence over what happens to us. We spend our energy focusing on the wrong things, like resenting other people, when we could use that energy to advance in our goals.

For many years, I had played the blame game, evading personal responsibility for my actions. Around February, 2000, I was planning to get married for the first time. My wedding date was quickly approaching (July 29, 2000). With just a few months to plan what I considered my first and only dream wedding, I had to truly focus on what I considered most important; to me that was my "big day". Unfortunately, each month leading up to my wedding day I saw problems in the relationship manifesting from the very beginning, but I refused to accept what I saw and got married anyway.

I did everything I could to avoid and dodge what I didn't want to face or deal with, and that was my own actions. I used every reason or excuse I could think of to curse, argue, and even physically fight my soon-to-be new husband. I often used those reasons as an excuse to stay mad, mean and violent.

I blamed my now ex-husband for everything that wasn't going right in our home or in our finances. Although he struggled with drug addiction throughout our entire relationship, I used all of his personal struggles as an excuse to allow me to constantly behave badly. Yes, maybe his issues were a major reason, but I contributed as well. No one made me who I was, other than me and my actions.

My husband would often wake up at the crack of dawn, prepare for work and leave the house by 7am (sometimes earlier) to go to work from 8am until 4:30 pm. His work shift may have ended around the same time as every other average employed American, but it was very common for him to drag in the back door in the late evening, sometimes as late as midnight. In fact, I never expected him to arrive home before dark, regardless of the season.

I already knew that this was his uninterrupted routine throughout our entire relationship, but my excuses to go on a rampage were endless. I would hoop, holler, curse and carry on every single day.

My favorite two words were "if" and "but". I would say things like, "If he didn't run the streets all the time, I wouldn't do this or that." "If he didn't spend all of his money everywhere but home, I wouldn't do this or that." Making excuses is similar to blaming others, except it involves blaming circumstances instead of people.

For fifteen long years, I lived by excuse after excuse; fifteen long years of awful behavior, which kept me going up and down the same mountains over and over again. I am not saying that everything was my fault, but I chose to be in that situation and to repeatedly make bad decisions. My stubbornness and refusal to face the truth kept me from repenting, which kept God from helping me.

1 John 1:8-10 (MSG) says, "If we claim that we're free of sin, we're only fooling ourselves. A claim like that is errant nonsense. On the other hand, if we admit our sins—make a clean breast of them—he won't let us down; he'll be true to himself. He'll forgive and purge us of all wrongdoing. If we claim that we've never

sinned, we out-and-out contradict God—make a liar out of him. A claim like that only shows off our ignorance of God."

Blaming had become a habit for me and made things appear worse than they really were. It distracted me from all the good things that were happening in my life. The closer I got to God the more I accepted responsibility and stopped blaming others. When I focused more on developing a reputation for being a person who accepted responsibility for my own actions, people often simply ignored the fact that I made a mistake altogether.

God showed me my mess on the inside that I needed to work on cleaning up. He confirmed that the hurt would not stop until I took responsibility for my own life. It was time for me to stop trying to escape from my life and face what was going on so that the world and new options were opened up for me. Abraham Lincoln said, "You cannot escape the responsibility of tomorrow by evading it today."

Putting the responsibility of resolving my negative emotions and healing my pain on someone else only allowed me to give away my personal power, and lose control over my life. It put me in a place of complaining. Making tons of excuses and doing enough complaining helped me lose motivation to do anything about my situation. There were so many days when I would lay down and just cry until I would finally fall asleep—only to wake up and relive what I considered hell all over again.

The more I attempted to avoid and delay holding myself accountable the more power I lost. The longer I allowed myself to be disempowering the more intense and greater the pain and loss of energy became. I eventually fell into a state of depression. No matter how happy I wanted and hoped to be, I was deeply miserable. I often tried doing things that motivated me and just when I thought I was starting to feel better, I would suddenly burst into tears.

Although my flesh would have a fit, I made a decision to admit my wrongs and stop pointing the finger elsewhere. I refused to stay trapped in wrong behavior patterns and continue postponing taking responsibility.

No more rationalizing to myself, I just accepted reality. I observed that I had hurt my own self and my own life. I felt unbearable pain, which doesn't feel good. Experiencing this level of pain firsthand made me less prone to repeating the same mistakes.

Taking responsibility eventually made me feel better about myself and made tough situations become easier to cope with. Taking action had become natural to me. I found the lessons and counted them as blessings.

The more I accepted my own mess and worked on it the more peace I had. The more peace I had the easier it was for me to wholeheartedly find a genuine connection with God. It was in that peace that I found the true me and learned to hear the voice of God.

Hearing His voice allowed me to hear and acknowledge the truth about what I had done to contribute to the destruction of my marriage and how I was negatively influencing my own children. I repented and stopped finding excuses and trying to justify my actions. God completely forgave me.

It was then that I learned that my justification is found only in Jesus Christ and I am made right with God after sinning by the blood of Jesus.

When you blame others, you give them the freedom to create your life the way they want it to be. You give the power and control to whomever and wherever you point the finger. Some think that they are holding others accountable, but there is a thin line between holding someone accountable and blaming them. You must understand the difference between the two, because blaming never works.

Be willing to take conscious control of your responses and circumstances in your life. What you seek of others is only to be found within yourself, for you are the source of your expectations not the recipient of some others responsibility to fulfill. What you have already done with your life and what you do in the future is up to you.

You must start caring for yourself in ways that strengthen, support, nurture and nourish your overall well-being. Once you do that, you begin taking charge of your life and have more positive energy to create something new for yourself. You begin to develop a natural feeling of deserving more and it helps to build your self-esteem, as you gain control of what happens in your life. Get over it and rise with a smile. Soon you will be healed and your wounds will only be past memories.

**(Psalm 32: 3-4 MSG)** "When I kept it all inside, my bones turned into powder, my words became daylong groans. The pressure never let up; all the juices of my life dried up."

## **Chapter Checkpoint:**

What are you tolerating but blaming on others?

How do you deal with being hurt or rejected by others?

What steps do you take to make sure that you are holding yourself accountable or responsible for your own actions?

What will you do to resolve any unresolved resentment or bitterness?

# Chapter 3
## *Pitiful or Powerful*

Self-pity occurs if one becomes frustrated, feels hopeless, thinks achieving goals is impossible, is disappointed, set back or defeated. Painful events live in your memory and open your mind to negative thoughts. "No one has suffered as I suffer, this is totally unfair, I deserve to be rewarded for my pain and retaliation is my right!" You are not in any way concerned for anyone other than yourself.

Often, the root of self-pity lies in this predicament; we become resentful of others because they are able to do what we wish we could do, or they are unable to do what we want them to do. No one has done anything to us, but we believe they have. Therefore, we think mean and nasty thoughts and take them for truths that make us feel pained, offended, upset and bitter. In reality, we are resenting our commitment to being ourselves.

Every human is prone to self-pity, including ministry leaders, but it is not of

God. 2 Corinthians 6:3-5 (NIV) says, "We put no stumbling block in anyone's path, so that our ministry will not be discredited. Rather, as servants of God we commend ourselves in every way: in great endurance; in troubles, hardships and distresses; in beatings, imprisonments and riots; in hard work, sleepless nights and hunger;"

As a believer, God wants you to recognize and prepare for the stressful conditions that accompany your walk with Him, regardless of who you are. No one is exempt from tough times, trials or tribulations.

The grand intention of self-pity is to spread unhappiness by making a person experience feelings of intense sorrow for their self, seeking mercy from other people. Sometimes this leaves the pitied depressed and psychologically harmed, which makes it hard for the person to stay in the present moment, be appreciative, creative and feel a connection to other people.

Self-pity can be a hidden impediment to advancing in life. There are times when you may be really working hard to accomplish something and suddenly you hit a stumbling block. You instantly feel flattened and have a hard time resisting the desire to give up.

Once self-pity settles over you, it's hard to get it off of you but it's possible. You will need to be more aware of when it's creeping up on you. Start challenging yourself to stop as soon as you realize that your thought process is negative. Redirect your thinking and change your self-talk. It will take time and you may still make the mistake of getting caught up in self-pity, but each time you get it wrong is one step toward getting it right.

Take back your personal power by focusing on how you have been blessed and acknowledging what is going right, instead of everything going wrong. Even if you must journal it, acknowledge when you do something positive, even if you don't get your desired result. It will help re-program your thought patterns.

Meditating can also help to break you out of the self-pity cycle. Although it requires lots of patience, persistence and self-discipline, meditating leads to greater self-awareness.

I have been in lots of pain, but I have also caused a lot of pain. I have been betrayed, but I have also betrayed. Every person who has experienced any hurt has been both a victim and a culprit. Every person is flawed and we can't change that. The more you face self-pity and begin to accept yourself the sooner you will see the self-transformation.

It's not what actually hurt you that caused you to feel sorry for yourself, it's the feelings that resulted from what happened that impact you the most. These feelings lead to discouragement, which makes you imprisoned by it. You then come to terms with feeling sorry for yourself.

If you are being plagued by self-pity, pray and ask God to help you conquer it. Then believe that He will change things on your behalf. Once you realize that God is working within you, your past wounds will become your future wisdom. Choose not to let your feelings harm you because you can't allow the things that have happened in life to paralyze you.

If you ever want to truly free yourself from self-pity, you must start seeing every issue or struggle as another step towards greatness. Life is tough and sometimes you must discover the strength within to force yourself to keep moving forward in order to overcome the pain of what has taken place in your life.

Once you find that inner strength, you can embrace your pains as springboards for development by understanding that they were just a part of the process and opportunities to be better. If you do that, you will be in the process of releasing yourself from the pain associated with your memory of them.

Your tears will be inevitable, but they are nothing to be ashamed of. Your tears are a testament to the courage needed to persevere through severe suffering without losing hope. Feel relaxed in knowing that you have been divinely empowered to press through the pain that comes as you pursue a more promising future.

Change the way you think about the events that have taken place in your life. If you can change the way you think, your life will begin to change, which is critical to growth, progress and healing. Although change is a process, it's also a catalyst for growth.

Instead of feeling guilty, bitter or regretting things that have happened, see them as opportunities to forgive, let go and use your life story as a testimony to minister to others. We have all experienced some level of joy and pain, and the enemy will use the people you love and relationships that God meant for our good to keep us in bondage and destroy us.

When guilt and bitterness assail you, stay in prayer and allow God's Word to penetrate in the areas where you feel pained. His Word can comfort you as you begin your process of healing. God can perform miracles.

**(1 Thessalonians 5:18 NIV)** "Give thanks in all circumstances; for this is God's will for you in Christ Jesus."

## **Chapter Checkpoint:**

Do you feel like a victim? If so, why?

Do you mull and muse over your problems constantly? If so, why?

How do you feel about what life has dealt you?

What do you find hard to accept in your life? What are you doing to help your situation?

# Chapter 4
## *Your Greatest Enemy*

In life we are often challenged and overcome by distress and become disheartened, allowing our spiritual self to disengage with our life source, God. We are more challenged by ourselves than we realize, and this makes us our own greatest enemy.

Much of the self-hate and tireless frustration that we experience stems from our own hands. We allow deep feelings of personal inadequacy to hold us back and limit our true potential, worrying about what others will think or say. In return, we rarely make decisions that lead us closer to realizing the plans that God has for us.

There was a point in my life when I was my own worst critic. Before anyone could criticize me, I had already criticized myself. Nothing I did was ever good enough to me. After reflecting on all that I had accomplished, I asked myself, "Am I living up to my own expectations or trying to live up to someone else's expectations?" My answer was found in the latter category.

Finally, I did some mental cleaning and reconnected with what I desired and the *'real me'*. Rediscovering who I really am makes me feel so much better. It reminds me to stop forcing myself to see the negative in every situation, and to celebrate all of my wins regardless of how big or small they may be. It reminds me that God created me to be a winner.

God has given us the power to make decisions that will change our positions and reverse the negative situations in which we live. It's up to us to determine our happiness and failures and decide how we will live our lives. We must live life in the present, focusing on creating a better today.

Every person is different. How many times have you heard that who you become is based on heredity? How many times have you heard that you can't ever be successful if you don't have this degree or that degree? You are not barred from achieving greatness because of the passing on of physical or mental characteristics genetically from a previous generation, ancestry or lack of education. You can choose to pursue greatness regardless of where you were born or how you were raised.

When you accept other people's perceptions of who you are and what you are capable of achieving, you doubt yourself and open yourself up to feeling victimized and helpless. When you are in that state, you are hard to pull up. It's time to get up, pull off the armored mask that you use for protection and be you.

Don't allow yourself to suffer due to someone else's opinion of you. Reveal your authentic self and don't worry about being rejected, judged or misunderstood. Just because they don't know who you are doesn't mean that you don't know who you are.

Our lack of confidence causes us to defend or condone why we won't embrace the greatness within us. We are always finding reasons to hold us back from what we fear—the unknown. Our inner self tells us it's too hard. Our inner self tells us it's too risky. Well, that's the best time to fight through the horror because the excitement builds from not knowing what's going to happen.

Most of the time we know we can accomplish what we wish but our lack of confidence increases our level of doubt. We put ourselves through a tragic process that puts us against our own self. That's when we limit our ability to succeed and use our personal power. We were never intended to live tiny and limited but to grow into the immense potential the entire kingdom offers.

If we never face and deal with our enemy—ourselves— it will wear us down because it follows us everywhere we go. It will remind us of all of the hard places in life that we have been, causing us to filter out and forget about the good things in life. We fail to appreciate the small things because they just aren't big enough. We take too much for granted instead of appreciating that this moment is far better than it could have been.

Most of the time we are praying for the promise but don't want to go through the process. We want things to come easy, forgetting that if it were easy everyone else would have it too. Why would we receive the promise if we don't even want it bad enough to take the necessary actions or steps to get it?

We look for people to believe in our dream but we don't believe in ourselves. We get upset because other people won't invest in us but we won't even invest in ourselves. Most of the time we self-injure ourselves and we are the reason for our own downfalls and failures but fail to recognize it. It's time to stop hiding from everything in life worth attaining.

Life is filled with questions, but when we refuse to give the power of our thinking to the positive influences in our lives we are our own worst critics and we often over analyze things. We seem to be working toward some goal that seems elusive.

We berate ourselves, lose sight of our successes and eventually lose ourselves in the process, not understanding that we are our greatest asset and all the happiness we seek is present if we are prepared to notice it.

If we choose to live our lives consciously and focus on the good, we can emotionally heal. Our circumstances change when we change and we can change whenever we wish. When we change, we have the opportunity to extend and expand upon the success we already know. That's when our personal power grows stronger and we become more influential.

Embrace discomfort because that's when you become desperate to get through. When you are desperate, the journey to overcome your greatest fears and fight through your toughest challenges becomes more exciting. When you are excited, you refuse to just exist, you choose to live. That's when you begin to march confidently into the unknown in search of answers, which makes life more meaningful.

Don't stay comfortable in your routines of feeling sorry for yourself and hopeless. Open yourself to feeling free and full of hope. The way you routinely contemplate on what you know to be true and your thinking will be your reality. Control your thoughts and train your mindset to believe in you and make your dreams your reality.

You talk to yourself throughout the day. You hold conversations with yourself all day long. There's a mental monologue that runs in your head non-stop. Often, it consists of long speeches full of inaccurate statements about our own self. Why not allow what you speak to yourself to act as your catalyst to propel you to the next level in life? Why not use the power of positive thinking to help you thrive and build your empire?

No more emotionally paralyzing yourself by mulling over problems that you refused to address in your past. Don't be willing to continue persisting in the same destructive behaviors. Flip your thinking, stand up and confront them.

Never undermine your chances of succeeding by ignoring your own personal issues. As soon as you recognize an issue, tackle it straight on without hesitation. Never expect to lose, and keep a winning mindset. Go easy on yourself but keep going.

**(Proverbs 3:5-6 NIV)** "Trust in the LORD with all your heart and lean not on your own understanding; in all your ways submit to him, and he will make your paths straight."

## **Chapter Checkpoint:**

Do you expect constant contentment? If so, why?

Do you constantly doubt yourself? If so, why?

What successes have you had over the past year? Have you acknowledged them? If not, why not?

Do you find yourself constantly criticizing and finding faults in yourself? If so, why?

# Chapter 5
## *Unshackle Your Perspective*

Sometimes we are so focused on our obstacles and difficulties that we have boxed ourselves into a small corner. We become complacent living in that small corner of our potential, imprisoned in our past or current circumstances, preventing us from looking beyond the walls and fences between us and our dreams. Often, our perspectives shape our world and we must make proactive changes.

Numerous disappointments have contributed to conditioning us into having negative positions and ways of looking at ourselves. Although we should never force our own mistaken expectations and mandates on life, we think on the level of expecting the worst, so we aren't disappointed when it happens. Ex: We view something being delayed as something that ruined our entire plan. If our flight is cancelled or rescheduled for a later time, instead of using the time to get work done, study or make important phone calls, we interpret it as being stuck for hours.

We think that if something is taking longer than we anticipated, it's never going to work. The mandates that govern our expectations should not direct us toward unreasonable negative conclusions.

One of the most important steps toward living a positive life is being able to distinguish between what you imagine and what is actually happening in your life. Almost a hundred percent of all situations in life are less than perfect. Nothing is usually black or white, or all this and all that, which tends to make us focus on the negatives of life. It's hard for us to see that most of the great things that happen in our lives occur in a grey area between the extremes of happiness and destruction.

If you struggle with seeing the positives in your life, you must practice and learn how to focus your mind on changing your attitude or viewpoint on life. Whatever you focus on has the power to change your future and you should never focus on what you do not expect to see in your future. Your focus will either reveal your confidence or affirm your uncertainty.

Focusing your mind is like setting the sails on a sailboat. Your thoughts should flow smoothly across your mind. Train your brain to go in a different direction when negative thoughts come and empower your perspective by balancing your focus. It can actually help improve your mood and decision-making abilities.

Wherever your focus your mind, talents, abilities and emotions will follow. Examine not only the worst case scenario but the best case scenario as well. This will give your mind more options to consider and help reduce extreme emotions. Allow your emotions to fuel you, stop seeing the old water jar as half empty, have more zeal and positivity, and notice how much clearer and realistically you begin to see things.

Make new choices to create your life again. You are always one decision away from succeeding, fulfilling your purpose and maximizing your potential. Sometimes you search far and wide to discover your purpose but if you will open your mind, heart, and ears to hear, you will find that it's right in front of you.

You must concentrate on hearing God's voice and master the art of concentration. Doing so will give you power over your life, but it's up to you to press in to hear what God has purposed for you and then obey what you hear from Him. Refuse to limit yourself by allowing your perspective to cloud your judgment. Explore every opportunity and lift every lid before you.

Everything that you are going through has a purpose, even if you don't understand it. God planned your being to be preserved by your spirit and your spirit to be preserved by hope in Him. Hope is a powerful force and you should latch on to it anywhere you can find it. It's an anchor and life-saving rope used to rescue you in times of difficulty. Make sure your hope is in an anchor, not a ship sailing away.

Feel peace in knowing that you can change your mood in an instant by breaking away from old thinking patterns and changing your perspective. First you must acknowledge that you choose and form your own perspectives. Therefore, you have the freedom to choose to change them into positive ones. If you focus on breaking old habits and being stuck in old ways, you will begin to see solutions to your frustrations that you had not seen before.

Soon you will begin to view things from a new window and understand that some things are beyond your control. If it's beyond your control, you cannot let it consume you. Old habits and ways corrupt your ability to strive for greatness in your life. It's time to heal the hole in your soul!

**(Romans 8:28 NIV)** "And we know that in all things God works for the good of those who love him, who have been called according to his purpose."

## **Chapter Checkpoint**

How do you perceive things when they don't go as planned?

How do you focus your mind on seeing the positive even in negative situations?

What do you do to ensure that you have control of your own personal power?

What action have you taken to break old habits and ways?

## Chapter 6
### *Think About What You're Thinking About*

Scientists have found that the average person thinks about 50,000-70,000 thoughts each day. Did you know that the quality of your life begins and ends with your thoughts? There is a saying, "He who controls his mind, controls his life." I believe that the opposite of that statement is equally true…He who doesn't control his mind has no control over his life.

Your thoughts determine who you are, what you do, and what you will or will not accomplish in life. Your thoughts can tie you down, refusing to allow you to go any further than where you are. At the end of the day, your thoughts determine your destiny. You have to be a good thinker if you are going to make good choices in your life.

The word 'thought' is defined as a mental picture of something such as a future or possible event. It's an expectation or hope that something will happen. What we think is often expressed in our speaking and reaches the ears of others. What we say communicates what's going on in our minds.

We share our feelings and our dreams through speaking and it impacts how we feel and how we make others feel. Our feelings are closely intertwined with our thoughts. Our hearts work off of our minds. We access our heart and then direct it by focusing our thoughts and inclining our feelings.

Take a look at everything around you. It's all energy. The buildings, the oceans, the mountains, the moon, the stars and even the solar system; they are all a form of energy. Your body and mind is also a form of energy.

Pay close attention to your daily energy. Think about the times when you were very confident that you could and would do something. Everything seemed to work out good and was rather exciting. The reason everything went well was because of your positive energy.

Remember the times when you felt down and depressed and everything seemed to go wrong? It was your low and negative energy that attracted equally negative situations to you. It's the law of attraction and it's always at work. Your mind is the magnet that attracts everything you experience in life.

Thinking is something we all do naturally. I have experienced unfortunate situations in life, and have found myself thinking and thinking. The more I would think, the worse my thinking would get. I would have one thought, then another one, and it became a continuous process. My mind jumped restlessly, not allowing me to think properly. I often over-interpreted what had happened, failing to realize that my thoughts were not always true.

When I was in my early to late twenties, there seemed to be a continuing dialogue of thoughts in my mind. There were multiple instances where my thoughts would keep me awake and in a state of fear. Sometimes I would think about an upcoming eviction notice with no plan of how my rent would be paid. Other times, I would think about if I received a phone call in reference to something tragic happening to my husband and the impact it would have on me and the children. My mind was constantly rolling, and it began negatively affecting me in almost every area of my life. It became destructive.

I had no control of my thoughts, so my only choice was to believe them. I had no idea of how to manage them, and that is why the quality of life that I desired could not be produced.

My negative thoughts caused me to criticize, have preconceived ideas, be judgmental, and overall feel very annoyed. The more those thoughts presented themselves, the more I let go of my own personal power. My negative mindset often ruined some of the most beautiful days.

I was losing myself to worry and fear, until I finally realized that I had to open my eyes to look at things differently, and live differently. I had to find more positive things to think about. When negative thoughts crossed my mind, I would ask myself "What is the worst thing that can happen?" I then started preparing to accept it, and began the practice of commanding myself to say "stop."

The direct command helped interrupt my negative thinking and I started creating positive thinking habits. My subconscious mind was in process of being reprogrammed. When my thoughts started changing, my feelings began to change as well. The triggers that set off negative feelings were eliminated.

It's important that we focus on creating a habit of thinking positive at all times. A habit is an action we do regularly, often without thinking. It's just what we do. When we focus on creating a habit to think positively, we will eventually do it unconsciously. That habit is beneficial and good discipline.

Our minds are our best asset and we can learn how to interrupt any negative thoughts, shifting them to positive. Focusing your thoughts in a positive manner expands your thinking and lifts the limitations on your achievements. Developing powerful thought habits can super charge your journey to destiny. You can then harness and use them for maximum results.

Most of the time, you are not consciously aware of what you are thinking about and often your thoughts control how you are feeling at that given moment. Could it be that you are feeling afraid? Are you feeling overwhelmed? Are you feeling nervous? The event that is making you feel that way is usually just the vehicle your mind is using to create the emotional state.

Be mindful of your thoughts and soon as you recognize that you are having negative thoughts you should stop for a few minutes, identify the thoughts and start changing them. Being mindful allows you take deliberate action that you consider to be in your best interest.

When you are able to immediately start changing your thoughts, you have then started training yourself to be the observer of your mind. Passing thoughts are no longer controlling it.

It's vital that you train your mind by disciplining it think positive so that it's not going on its own tangent and being rebellious. If you make discipline a routine, it will accept whatever you require of it.

When negative thinking tries to invade your mind, you must focus on redirecting it toward the right objects of trust. In other words, your mind must be redirected to having positive thoughts. If you want to be happy, your trust and mind must be set in the right direction.

When you wake up in the morning, you have two choices. One is a positive mental attitude, and one is a negative mental attitude. Waking up and deciding to be positive prepares your mind to be ready to face daily challenges.

Sometimes, having positive thoughts require concentration. Concentration is not automatic. It's a learned skill which enables you to fix your attention on one single thought or subject, while at the same time excluding from your awareness everything else. Concentration prevents scattering your efforts, conserves your energy, and do not dissipate them on irrelevant thoughts or activities.

While most people would agree that concentration is a benefit to controlling your thinking, most are not motivated or focused on making it stronger. Developing the power of concentration will give you peace of mind, inner strength and happiness, and overall improve your self confidence.

**(Romans 12:2 NIV)** Do not conform to the pattern of this world, but be transformed by the renewing of your mind. Then you will be able to test and approve what God's will is—his good, pleasing and perfect will.

## Chapter Checkpoint

What is one of your biggest distractions?


What negatively affects your thinking?


How do you control your thinking?


How does your thinking affect your behavior?

# Chapter 7
## _Accept and Validate Yourself_

At birth, every person is in need of validation. Most parents love their children and offer them consistent validation. Parents validate feelings, talents, and intelligence. However, people who have never personally experienced being validated by their parents often have a difficult time with learning and knowing how to validate themselves. As a result, they make others their authority for what is right or wrong for them.

Unfortunately, we aren't living in the same world that we were born into. In fact, the world we live in is very "different." Therefore, if your plan is to live (not just exist) and experience great things in today's time, you are required to think and be "different." You are required to change your expectations of others validating you and learn to validate yourself.

Struggling to accept yourself causes you to lose track of who you really are. You gain a false confidence based on who you "want" to be. It's time to do what feels natural and remove the pressure from yourself, by following a path that's really meant for you. While it is a journey, it's time to learn to become more confident in your true self. It's time to understand that being yourself is all you need.

Self validation is not only possible, but necessary to being at peace and feeling worthy and happy. When you experience these feelings, there are no conditions. It makes you feel grateful for being who you are and alive because you are free to be your true self; the person you find easiest to be, and that's a huge relief.

Accepting yourself is really what matters most and when you accept yourself, it's much easier to follow your heart and do what's more important to you. It starts with valuing your own feelings and trusting your inner knowing, rather than seeking validation from others. With time and patience, you can learn to value and accept yourself.

I have noticed that when my mind is much clearer, it's easier for me to focus on what I want and believe for myself. Focusing on what I want leaves so much room for my heart to speak to me. My heart tells me who I want to be and what I want to do, not who others think I should be and what they want me to do.

I remember a time when I thought I was very happy. I loved myself, my family, and my job; so I thought. I worked in a call center as a Customer Service Representative. My job was professional and the atmosphere was very warm and family feeling. I would wake up each morning smiling and just being grateful as I prepared to go to work. During my early morning rides to work, I listened to motivational speakers to get my day started and loved when I entered the building being greeted by other smiling faces.

After 9 months on the job, I was promoted to a Quality Assurance Lead position without even applying or expressing interest. Things were going really well, and people often told me that I was a great fit for the position because I was very knowledgeable and did the job well. What a great feeling. I had no idea that those feelings would soon wear off.

After about a year on the job, I really began to feel bored and uninspired in my position, but I continued to convince myself that I loved it. I was building great relationships and there was no reason for me to feel anything other than happy. I started thinking, "Maybe I am not using my spare time wisely and that's why I feel so unfulfilled."

Soon after, I discovered that I was very passionate about helping others enhance the quality of their lives. I started planning my evenings and weekends around networking with other people at empowerment events, speaking and enjoying using my spare time to do it.

With lots of excitement, I shared with family and friends my desire to help others and to start a women's empowerment organization to educate and empower people globally. Most told me how great they thought the idea was and before I knew it, I was starting to like organizing seminars and workshops much better than my full-time job. I wasn't getting paid for it. In fact, I was spending tons of money to do it, but it didn't matter to me. My passion wouldn't allow me to focus on money.

As time went by, I had the community getting involved. Unfortunately, the expectation of me grew and I did not have all of the answers, nor did I know the people who did. I really needed a strong support team, which I did not have. Regardless of my efforts to make positive changes in the community, I just couldn't seem to get my plane off of the ground.

Everyone thought it was a great idea, but they thought the idea of me spending more time trying to be promoted on my job made much more sense than trying to build a team and organization of people to help with my idea of helping other people. The more I tried, the less support I had. People had their own agendas and after work, they were just too tired to commit to helping with anything else.

Although, I never gave up, I knew that my family and friends expected me to excel on the job, not in starting a business. In their minds, it was way too much work and too hard. I eventually bought in to their thoughts and opinions and continued to try and reignite my love for my job.

I knew there was little to no room for growth or expansion, but I had settled for sticking and staying because that's what I was expected to do. I didn't want my family and friends to completely lose hope in me and give up on me, so I was determined to make the job work. I thought to myself, "Whatever makes my family happy is what makes me happy."

In five short years, I had witnessed 4 layoffs. Each time, my family and I would thank God that I was not one of the people who lost their jobs. No one ever encouraged me to try anything different. They just told me to stay in prayer and God would make everything on my job ok.

Watching colleagues that I had built great relationships with, walk out of the building with tears rolling down their faces after the layoffs caused me to be extremely fearful. I would have unexpected panic attacks after each layoff, but the promises (from management) of no more future layoffs kept me hanging in there.

I never felt secure, but I just couldn't muster the courage to be honest enough with my family and tell them that I wanted to quit, but I needed their help and support. I wanted to quit, but I needed their encouragement. I wanted to quit, but I needed them to really help me pursue my God given purpose. I just wanted to "quit". I automatically knew that if I told them that, their idea of my dream of being an entrepreneur or business owner would be me sitting at home online, on the couch, in my pajamas all day long. I knew they couldn't actually visualize me being successful.

I was so afraid to let them in on my hidden secret of wanting to proactively pursue my own dream instead of building someone else's. After all, I had a family to feed. I felt forced to keep asking myself, "How can I just quit this job that my family is expecting me to bring home a paycheck from every two weeks?"

After five and a half years on the job, I was finally called into a small empty office and told that my services were no longer needed. Even after spending more than a half decade devoting my time and work, they asked me to leave the building for good, find a way to get money elsewhere, and figure out how to provide health insurance for my family. Those benefits were no longer available to me. They suddenly snatched my "security blanket" and there was nothing I could do about it. What a major wake-up call that was for me.

For some reason, I wasn't upset at all. Others who had lost their jobs were crying and sad, but all I could think to myself was "How come I waited for this?" "How come I didn't just find a way to get my business off of the ground?" "Why did I give up my personal power to other people?" After all, I was exactly where people expected me to be with my own business; without income.

I immediately had a feeling that it was the perfect time for me to do what my heart was truly connected to. Again, I shared my hopes and dreams with my immediate family. Although I had no job, they never gave me any indication that they would support me, were in my corner or even approved of my feelings. Conversing with them was very difficult. They had the "You need a job" look on their faces.

I soon realized that regardless of how much I explained, they still thought the safety of a 9 to 5 was best. It wasn't that they didn't want me to do it at all, but they didn't believe that they could create their own business and live a freelance life, so how could I? Truthfully, I understood that there was nothing secure about another person writing my checks for me, but they didn't.

It was then that I realized that just because my family and friends didn't understand my dream and felt like I needed a job, there was no reason for me to continue living in fear of hurting their feelings. What they thought about me could not diminish the quality of my life, but what I thought about myself. I was done with talking myself out of making the attempt to go after what I really wanted.

I finally made a decision to accept and approve myself. There was no way I could make any progress if I didn't accept myself. It was no longer acceptable to allow others to determine my worth, value and significance in life. That's a dangerous position to be in.

I became determined to develop strength, courage and motivation to make a new start. I knew that what I did from that moment forward was what was going to count. I was no longer afraid of experiencing a failure or setback. Although the setback may be an experience, it will not be a reflection of my personal worth and I will still experience victories.

Don't spend your time abandoning yourself while trying to please other people. The more you care for yourself, the more inner peace and confidence you have. You become more independent and begin to follow your own path and create your own happiness.

View each moment with new eyes, new potentials and turn your life into what you want it to be. The more you validate yourself, the more you keep your self-esteem rooted internally. It will not be all rainbows and sunshine, but keep reaching for your peak and shine when you get to the top.

You are greatness filled with purpose but the most important person that needs to know that is YOU! Accept that you are amazing, and snatch back your personal power!

**(Galatians 1:10 NIV)** "Am I now trying to win the approval of human beings, or of God? Or am I trying to please people? If I were still trying to please people, I would not be a servant of Christ

## **Chapter Checkpoint**

How important is self-validation to you?

Other than yourself, who are you always trying to please and why?

What are you doing to create the life you desire to live?

What have you done for yourself that makes your really proud?

# Chapter 8
## _Who's the Judge?_

It's very normal to want to be liked by others. In fact, seclusion is dangerous for our mental health. But if you break faith with yourself to change the feelings or opinions of others, problems are caused that are at least as bad if not worse.

Certain emotions arise when we wonder what other people think of us. We want to have pleasant experiences with everyone, of course and our fear of other peoples negative opinions are way too high. Sometimes we overestimate how much and how badly others think of us.

It's extremely important for us to know how we feel about ourselves. It's totally up to us to be responsible for defining ourselves and understand who we are so that we may live according to that truth. If we are always worrying about being liked, we eventually adapt a people pleasing mentality. We end up giving away our personal power to maintain a positive image to others.

Although most people don't want to be perceived as a bad person, caring too much about what others think can prevent them from building their dream life. Never should another person's thoughts of you or estimation of your abilities become more important than your own. Depending too much on someone else's opinion of you will force you to neglect and honor your own agenda and deny your own value.

One can never live authentically, be healed with no leaks, punctures or wounds if they aren't grounded internally in their own values. Living authentically will keep you on your path to greatness or success and you will begin to live a more purposeful and fulfilling life. Only you can chart the journey to living free and clear of allowing someone else's opinions to dictate how your life progresses.

Focus on the image of the person that you vision yourself to be, and don't be distracted listening to others. Be who you are without allowing the external pressure and demands of other people who are close to you or society to force you into a false mold. Honor your own agenda, enforce your own values, find your voice and dare to use it. Make your potential known without looking for validation or approval. Approve yourself, regardless.

I remember a time in my life where I felt like I kept going in a circle. I was beginning to feel paralyzed in all of my efforts to move forward. It was really because I wasn't clear on what I wanted in life and as a result, my efforts were depleting me.

I spent such a long time chasing after the goals without having a clear vision or purpose. I began to doubt myself and wondering if my walk was in vain. I was slowly losing all self-motivation and relying on the encouragement and compliments of others to temporarily keep me going, because I had never spent time getting to know who I really was and what my true purpose in life was. I had absolutely no idea of what I stood for and what my priorities in life were.

I had developed a terrible strategy of needing approval and it wasn't working very well. My 'people pleaser' strategy was failing tremendously and I didn't even realize it. I began to sabotage my own self and ask "Should I really be doing this?" "Can I really be successful at this?" "Should I just go ahead and quit?" After all, I just wanted one person (besides myself) to tell me I could do it.

I shared my challenges and how I was struggling with close friends and family members. I began to open up about my true feelings of being tired of trying to run a successful business and feeling so alone doing it. I had become desperate for praise from my family and friends and slowly became bitter and resentful when I didn't get it.

As time passed, I started doing some true soul searching to get to know who I was and what I stood for. The more I learned about myself, the more independent I became. I had soon become completely independent of the good or the bad opinions of others and started reaching my goals much easier and faster.

My soul was made whole and I started making self-honoring choices and standing firmly in who I am in my core. I was no longer triggered by someone else's praise. I took my own opinions more seriously and took my dreams and visions out of the hands of randomness, out of the imagination of other people.

I had finally realized that no other human being could offer me fulfillment and it was ok if I didn't get the response or compliment that I wanted or felt I desired. If I was going to live an extraordinary life, I had to let go of depending on random circumstances.

When I thought of all of the successful artists and people in the world who were told that their work was awful or that they would never make it, but later went on to be very successful I became ok with being rejected. I encourage you to come to terms with everyone not liking you because if everyone likes you, you're probably not being true to yourself.

You were created to be authentic and it's ok to be the odd one or the one who doesn't seem to fit in. It's ok to be the one who everyone thinks is foolish. If it were meant for everyone to think alike, we wouldn't be able to think critically and develop creative solutions.

Don't allow people to cut you down and belittle you. Stop hiding everything that is unique about you just to wear a mask, because rejection helps to build tougher skin. If you ever want to be a visionary and build your dreams, you must be authentic and have tough skin. You must trust your own vision before the rest of the world sees it. If you are living authentically, you will not only change your life, you will be poised to change the world.

**(Jeremiah 1:5 NIV)** "Before I formed you in the womb I knew you, before you were born I set you apart; I appointed you as a prophet to the nations."

## **Chapter Checkpoint**

How important is it to you that you are perceived as a good person to others? Why?

How important is it for you to be authentic? Why?

Name a time when you valued someone else's opinion of you more than you valued your own

Define yourself and what you stand for

## Chapter 9
## _Much Power Lies Within Your Mental Strength_

Life is extremely tough and sometimes our energy is drained from ruminating about things we can't control. Every person possesses the will to push themselves beyond discomfort and pain, but our emotional experiences can cause our core beliefs to be inaccurate. We struggle to make the best choices when responding to difficult situations because we must learn to tolerate discomfort.

That all begins with having a measure of individual resilience and confidence. In other words, we must become mentally strong if we ever want to reach new heights and become the person we wish to become.

I remember a time when I was in a really dark place in my life. I had gone through a period where things were really getting tough in my relationship with family and my finances. Although I had many painful experiences, this particular time had me so tied up in my head with stress, anger, and pain that I was not only mentally sick, but I had become physically sick. At this point, I was a powerless player to the enemy's game.

Sadly, I had given more brain power to areas of my life that didn't deserve it, and I couldn't seem to find strength while under stress. Things went all the way wrong and I went with them. I started laying around feeling sorry for myself and began hosting my own pity parties.

Soon after, I realized that I had fallen into a state of depression and my negative thoughts and feelings had power that was very much alive. My interest in what I once enjoyed began to fade away, along with my energy to do anything. I was hardly ever in a mood good enough to enjoy life, because I was storing away lots of issues which caused me to bottle up my emotions and become miserable.

One day, it suddenly hit me. I needed to use my pain as an instrument for my greatest growth, but how? How do I learn to grow and build myself from my experiences? By building my mental strength, which would help me to fight through obstacles and keep pushing until I reach my goals.

The more I focused on building my mental strength, the more I noticed I had my own inner drive that pushed me to improve and work on myself. My sense of direction became deeply internalized and I no longer had to worry about being lost. It had become easier to stay motivated even during the most challenging times, because I was no longer looking for encouragement from others.

In order to prevent giving away your personal power you must practice and be mindful of your mental strength. Make it a point of learning new habits to replace the old habits and occupying your mind with positive thoughts that will help you carry on when the world seems to have turned against you. If you ever want to overcome a difficult situation, mental toughness is mandatory. Discipline yourself so you can free yourself.

Learn the lessons from unexpected setbacks. Learn to keep your troubles in proper perspective without losing site of what you need to accomplish, and move on. You may still experience disappointments, but be accountable and positive each day and remember that nothing worthwhile in life is simple or easy to accomplish.

Focus on living in the moment and what's in front of you, and when times are tough put on your thinking caps and think of a creative way out. Remember that the most powerful tool that you have in your life is your mind. If you can get your mind out of a difficult situation, you can get your family, finances, health, prosperity, and heart out as well. It has been said that "A mind crowded with thoughts, is a weak mind. A mind free from thoughts is an extremely strong mind."

Choose to cultivate your mind just as you would choose which seeds to plant in a garden. It's your responsibility to believe and choose to plant peace, love, joy, compassion, discernment, wisdom, and self-care in your mind. You have the power to develop the mental strength to achieve whatever you desire.

If you can see yourself accomplish something in your mind, it is attainable. You just have to maintain your capacity to stay confident and deliver the same level of performance regardless of what you're feeling. Keep your attention on the long-term outcomes and be your absolute best while pushing yourself to the brink of whatever it is that you wish to accomplish.

**(Joshua 1:9 NIV)** "Have I not commanded you? Be strong and courageous. Do not be afraid; do not be discouraged, for the LORD your God will be with you wherever you go."

## **Chapter Checkpoint**

In your own words, define mental toughness

What can you do to help increase your mental strength?

What occupies your mind when you are faced with difficulty? Why?

How do you handle issues that are beyond your control?

## Chapter 10

## Appreciate Being Who God Created You To Be

In this final chapter, I would like to encourage you to love and enjoy being who God created you to be. You were intentionally created as one of God's 'rare' jewels and gems. God created you on purpose, for a purpose. Your life was no accident and he deliberately chose every single feature you have. You are perfected and completed in Him and He is proud of who He created you to be.

So often, our precious skills and passions that God has planted inside of us long ago get buried under layers of expectations and pressure. It's time to dig our sacred, beautiful collection of passions that God imprinted in our hearts out of the dirty hole of lies like these: "I don't look good enough," "I need the best car," "I don't have enough education," "I must have the biggest house" in order to be considered valuable. Those are lies that make you feel inadequate, and don't reflect what the Bible says is true. You were only meant, created, and commanded to be who you are.

God says that you are unconditionally loved and incredibly valuable and you must start focusing on what leads you closer to Him. Listening to lies only draw you farther from Him and never reflect an accurate perspective of your situation, which makes it hard for you to fulfill His purposes for your life.

Stop tangling yourself in tight little knots trying desperately to look like, speak like, walk like or be like someone else. That's not where the fullness of joy and meaning are found. God never intended for you to be the same as any other person, and you cannot be duplicated. Seeing yourself the way God does is the key to living the way He wants you to.

Every person on earth has their own individual set of strengths and weaknesses. No one is exempt. Don't act like anyone, other than who God made you to be. Regardless of how hard you try having the same strengths as others, they will always manifest differently through your own individual personalities. Learn to embrace who you are so that you can become all that God created you to be.

You have what it takes to fulfill God's purposes in your life. If you are going to rise above your circumstances and be all that He's created you to be, you must have the courage to live the life that He's called you to. God offers you an abundant life, but you must go in the direction that He's leading you.

Keep in mind that you should live to please God alone. Release the weight off of your shoulders and anticipate blessings. Be passionate about owning and protecting what God has given to you. Enjoy your journey, even if God seems silent when you're waiting for a prayer to be answered. Never wonder if you will survive in a world that's full of disappointment. God created you to live in peace.

Walk away from roles and expectations that other people have for you and allow freedom and grace to flood through you as you be who God's created you to be. Be well-prepared to serve God and others by finding ways to express your strengths that build up other people and benefit God's kingdom.

Take a look back over your life and find the threads of passion and identity you've carried throughout your whole life. Use that passion in ways in which you can best contribute to the world and honor God.

**(Psalm 139:13-14 NIV)** "For you created my inmost being; you knit me together in my mother's womb. I praise you because I am fearfully and wonderfully made; your works are wonderful, I know that full well."

**Chapter Checkpoint:**

What is one unique thing that God has created within you?

How can you take a step of faith to begin to walk in your God assigned purpose?

What will you do to help you rise above your circumstances and be all that God has created you to be?

What skills and passions have you always had and how will you use them?

## *Contact The Author:*

If you would like to request more copies or contact the author, please feel free to do so in writing at:

Andrea Freeman
P.O. Box 18151
Baltimore, MD 21220
info@authorandreafreeman.com

## *Author's Additional books available for purchase:*

No Barriers, No Limits

Think Up And Go Up

Thirty-One Days of Instant Inspiration

How We Made It Over

Irritated To Greatness

Blend Out To Stand Out

www.ingramcontent.com/pod-product-compliance
Lightning Source LLC
Chambersburg PA
CBHW071326040426
42444CB00009B/2092